A Game of Cat and Mouse

Michelle Watson

Illustrations by
Angel dela Peña

Print information available on the last page

Rev. date: 03/20/2015

To order additional copies of this book, contact:
Xlibris
1–888–795–4274
www.Xlibris.com
Orders@Xlibris.com

DEDICATION PAGE

You are the reason

OMAR
JAZZMAYN
LAVELL
LATRELL
LANCE
LAUREN
CHRISTIAN
KE'ONDRE
KHALE
A'LEYSIA

YOU ARE THE REASON I SMILE, YOU ARE THE REASON
I PRAY, YOU ARE THE REASON FOR MY LAUGHTER AND
FROM ME TO YOU I SAY, I LOVE ALL OF YOU VERY MUCH.

2

One day my dog came
in from outside. He
smelled really funny; I
did not know why.

My dad came in and then he said, "Why don't you give that dog a bath?"

I started the water, and
you should have seen
how quickly my dog
ran away from me.

I chased him all around
the house as if we were
a cat and a mouse.

My mother stopped me, and she said, "I thought you were giving the dog a bath. You guys are running around the house as if you were a cat and a mouse."

I tried to catch him, but no one believed how his little legs were faster than me.

My sister caught me, and she said, "Come get your doggy out of my bed. While you're playing like you're the cat, the dog's in my bed and taking a rest."

He saw me coming and
hit the door, running fast
across the kitchen floor.

And landed right
into his cage.

Now who's won the
cat–and–mouse game?

Printed in the United States
By Bookmasters